Leaders in My Community

Salima Alikhan, M.F.A.

Reader Consultants

Jennifer M. Lopez, M.S.Ed., NBCT
Senior Coordinator—History/Social Studies
Norfolk Public Schools

Tina Ristau, M.A., SLMS
Teacher Librarian
Waterloo Community School District

iCivics Consultants

Emma Humphries, Ph.D.
Chief Education Officer

Taylor Davis, M.T.
Director of Curriculum and Content

Natacha Scott, MAT
Director of Educator Engagement

Publishing Credits

Rachelle Cracchiolo, M.S.Ed., *Publisher*
Emily R. Smith, M.A.Ed., *VP of Content Development*
Véronique Bos, *Creative Director*
Dona Herweck Rice, *Senior Content Manager*
Dani Neiley, *Associate Content Specialist*
Fabiola Sepulveda, *Series Designer*

Image Credits: p10 Kansas Historical Society; p11 Allison Dinner/ZUMA
press/Newscom; p15 Saeed Khan/Contributor Getty Images; p17 Xochitl Neri;
p19 Kimberly Cabrera; p21 Martha Rial; p22 Cyrus McCrimmon/Getty Images
Contributor; p23 Giulio Napolitano/Shutterstock; pp24-25 Alen Thien/Shutterstock;
all other images from iStock and/or Shutterstock

Library of Congress Cataloging-in-Publication Data

Names: Alikhan, Salima, author.
Title: Leaders in the community / Salima Alikhan.
Description: Huntington Beach : Teacher Created Materials, 2021. | Includes
    index. | Audience: Grades 2-3 | Summary: "What are community leaders?
    They are people who help run our towns and cities. They help in big and
    small ways. They solve problems and create new ideas. Every community
    has leaders!"-- Provided by publisher.
Identifiers: LCCN 2020043593 (print) | LCCN 2020043594 (ebook) | ISBN
    9781087605067 (paperback) | ISBN 9781087619989 (ebook)
Subjects: LCSH: Civic leaders--Juvenile literature. | Community
    leadership--Juvenile literature.
Classification: LCC HN42 .A55 2021 (print) | LCC HN42 (ebook) | DDC
    303.3/4--dc23
LC record available at https://lccn.loc.gov/2020043593
LC ebook record available at https://lccn.loc.gov/2020043594

5482 Argosy Avenue
Huntington Beach, CA 92649-1039
www.tcmpub.com

ISBN 978-1-0876-0506-7

Table of Contents

What Is a Community Leader?

What is a leader? A leader helps people. All kinds of people can be leaders. Leaders can be loud or quiet. They can be funny or serious. They can be any gender. They can be any age.

Communities are places where people live and work together. Community leaders help solve problems. They help make schools, towns, and cities better.

Leaders work to keep us safe.

These leaders plant a new tree in their community.

Jump into Fiction

Help for the Fire Station!

The town fire station is old. The equipment is old too. Sometimes, the fire hoses break. The fire engines are too slow. It is hard for the firefighters to do their jobs.

Mayor Bell comes to see the firefighters. She agrees.

"Your equipment is too old," she says.

Mayor Bell meets with the City Council.

"The firefighters need new equipment," she tells them.

The council votes. They agree with the mayor. The firefighters will get brand new fire engines. They will get new equipment too.

The firefighters are grateful. This will help them do their jobs!

Back to Nonfiction

Types of Leaders

There are many types of leaders in a community.

Mayors

Cities and towns need someone to lead them. This leader is called the *mayor*. People may **vote** for the mayor. Or the mayor may be elected from within a council.

Mayors help make local laws. They make sure the city or town has money to fix things. Local people can ask the mayor to listen to what they need.

Leading the Way

The first female mayor was Susanna Madora Salter. She was elected to be mayor in Argonia, Kansas, in 1887.

Pete Buttigieg is a famous former mayor.

Think and Talk

Why should a leader listen to the public?

Coaches

Coaches lead sports teams. They teach people how to play sports. Coaches help athletes do their best. They help them build **confidence**. They help them learn **teamwork**.

Coaches need to be positive. They help their teams have fun. Athletes trust their coaches to make them better. Being a coach takes a lot of hard work.

Volunteers

Many people want to help their community. So they volunteer. This means they help without being paid. They help in all kinds of ways. Some might help at an animal **shelter**. Or, they might bring food to people who don't have enough to eat.

Volunteering is a good way to help your community.

Helping Animals

In 2020, fires in Australia put animals in danger. A lot of people volunteered. They helped keep the animals safe.

There are many ways people can volunteer. Some help at hospitals. Others help at **nursing homes**. They visit people or care for them.

Other volunteers restore parks or streams. They want to keep their communities nice. Some might plant flowers or trees. This helps keep the air clean.

Some ideas to help are easy to put into action. For example, people can pick up trash as they walk down a street. If each person did one small thing, it would help a lot!

Making a Difference with Art

Paige Miller is an artist. She volunteers at a theater to design and paint sets. She teaches kids and their parents how to do this, too.

Principals

A principal is the leader of a school. Teachers and students come to them for help. They make sure teachers have what they need. They help students feel excited to learn. Schools can be better places because of principals.

Principals are important school leaders.

Dog-Training Principal

Kimberly Cabrera is a school principal. She also trains guide dogs. She brings the dogs to school each day. Her students love to see the dogs. The dogs are students too!

Librarians

Being a librarian is a lot of work. Most people think librarians only help people find books. But they do more than that. They help people learn. They do **research** and read stories. They also help people with technology.

These students use technology from their library.

Hi-Tech Library

Ali Schilpp works in Maryland. She is a librarian. She made her library a special place. It is full of cool technology. There are even some robots!

Religious Leaders

Religious groups have leaders, too. These leaders help people **worship**. People come to them for help. They ask them for advice. These leaders may support other leaders in their community as well.

A woman studies to be a rabbi.

Religious leaders often help people outside of their communities too. They may put together trips to help people in other places. They may send supplies to people in need.

The Pope

One of the most well known religious leaders is the pope. This person is the leader of the Catholic Church.

Could You Do It?

Community leaders help people they lead. They make places better to live. They help keep people safe. They listen to people's needs. People trust these leaders. They show people how to take care of one another.

Do you have what it takes to be a leader?

Think and Talk

In this photo, can you tell who might be a leader?

Glossary

confidence—the belief in oneself or other people to do something

equipment—tools people need to do certain jobs

nursing homes—communities where older people who need care live together

religious—believing in God or gods and following the practices of a faith

research—searching for facts about something

shelter—a place that helps animals stay safe and find homes

teamwork—working well with other people

vote—to formally make a choice

worship—to pray to or honor something or someone

Index

Civics in Action

You can be a leader! You can volunteer. Good citizens help their communities. They get others to help too. Here is a way to do a good deed for your community.

1. Brainstorm ways you can volunteer.

2. Choose a project.

3. Plan what you will do.

4. Tell people about your project. Ask them to help.

5. Get to work!